Savvy

IT'S YOUR WORLD

A CRASH COURSE IN *Social Studies*

BY KATHIANN M. KOWALSKI

T0060851

Consultant:
Anne-Lise Halvorsen, PhD
Assistant Professor, College of Education
Michigan State University
East Lansing, Michigan

CAPSTONE PRESS
a capstone imprint

Savvy Books are published by Capstone Press,
1710 Roe Crest Drive, North Mankato, Minnesota 56003
www.capstonepub.com

Library of Congress Cataloging-in-Publication Data
Cataloging-in-publication information is on file with the Library of Congress.

ISBN 978-1-4914-0775-2 (library binding); ISBN 978-1-4914-0783-7 (paperback);
ISBN 978-1-4914-0779-0 (ebook PDF)

Editorial Credits
Jennifer Huston, editor; Heidi Thompson and Lori Bye, designers;
Gina Kammer, media researcher; Kathy McColley, production specialist

Photo Credits
Bridgeman Art Library: Private Collection/American School, (19th century), 40; Capstone: 49,
Capstone Studio: Karon Dubke, 31 (bottom); Corbis: Bettmann, 58; CriaImages.com: Jay Robert Nash
Collection, 8, 35, 43; Getty Images: Lonely Planet Images/Ariadne Van Zandbergen, 14, The Bridgeman
Art Library/French School, 32; iStockphotos: AndrisTkachenko, 21 (middle), RonTech2000, 56; Library
of Congress: Prints and Photographs Division (Gandhi and Meir), 55; National Archives and Records
Administration: War Production Board, 33; Newscom: akg-images, 37 (top left), Everett Collection,
44, 54, Photoshot, 59 (bottom); North Wind Picture Archives: 29; Shutterstock: 360b (Merkel), 55,
Anastasios71, 17 (middle), ANCH, 38 (right), Andrea Izzotti, 9 (right), (Psyche) 25, Andre Jabali, back
cover, Andresr (Persephone), 25, Anton_Ivanov, 39, Be Good, 7 (right), Bikeworldtravel (Eros), 25,
BonnieBC, 20 (bottom left), Dan Thornberg (flag), 40, David Fowler (Thatcher), 55, Deborah McCague,
37 (bottom right), Everett Collection, 45 (top), Geoffrey Kuchera, 36, Georgios Kollidas, 18, ifong, 38
(left), Im Perfect Lazybones (Hades), 24, jakkapan, 20 (top), Jeka, 7 (left), jmcdermottillo (pop art style
faces), cover and throughout, Jojje, 11 (top left), jorisvo, 31 (middle), Jos Post, 37 (middle right), J.
Quendag (Io), 24, julie deshaies, 38 (middle), kampolz, 6, khd (inset), 23, Kudryashka, (hand-drawn
colorful wave pattern), throughout, leonardo2011, 60, MAHATHIR MOHD YASIN, 26 (bottom),
Malgorzata Kistryn (Demeter), 25, Maxi_m (emoticons), 24, Mert Toker, 4, 23, michaeljung, 59 (top),
Mighty Sequoia Studio, 9 (bottom left), Mrivserg (Ares), 24, Muellek Josef (Athena), 24, Naaman
Abreu, 9 (top left), Nancy Bauer, 27 (top), Nico Traut, 20 (bottom right), Nuarevik, 12–13, Odua Images,
back cover, Olena Brodetska (Aphrodite), 25, Onur ERSIN, 46, PaNaS (Heracles), 24, patrimonio
designs ltd (Poseidon), 25, Paul Hakimata Photography, 5, perspectivestock, 19 (bottom), Rido, 28,
Robert Kneschke, 52, Rob Marmion, 34, Sergey Kamshylin, 11 (right), Sergey Rusakov, 21 (bottom),
Shyamalamuralinath, 26 (middle), S_L, 57, somartin, 45 (bottom), stefanel, 16, Stefanie Dollase-Berger,
27 (middle), Styve Reineck, 17 (bottom), Susan Law Cain, 42, tadijasavic, 21 (top), Timur Kulgarin
(Perseus), 25, tkachuk, 19 (top), Tudor Catalin Gheorghe (Zeus), 24, Tyler Olson, 53, Valentina Petrov
(Rousseff), 55, Victoria Kisel, 15, Zubada (Leda), 24, Zurijeta, 27 (bottom); SuperStock: Hero Images, 61
Design elements: Shutterstock

Primary source bibliography
Page 56—"All men are created equal" quote from the Declaration of Independence.
        http://memory.loc.gov/cgi-bin/query/r?ammem/bdsdcc:@field(DOCID+@lit(bdsdcc02101))
Page 56—Abraham Lincoln quote, August 1, 1858. www.abrahamlincolnonline.org/lincoln/speeches/quotes.htm
Page 59—Excerpt from Malala Yousafzai speech before the United Nations, July 12, 2013. www.youtube.com/
        watch?v=QRh_30C8l6Y

Printed in the United States of America in Stevens Point, Wisconsin.
032014   008092WZF14

Table of Contents

WEAVING IT ALL TOGETHER

You're a social person. You have family and friends. You belong to clubs. You go to school. You belong to bigger groups too—such as your family, school, community, and country. Your experiences with all these groups shape who you are, as does the time in which you live.

Do you have older friends or siblings on Facebook, Twitter, or another social network? Comments, posts, and pictures link them to their friends' groups and even to their friends' friends.

Other links connect you to more groups. For example, your family spans generations. Maybe you never knew your great-grandparents or their parents. Yet their choices affected your family and where you are today.

Social studies is about all sorts of groups throughout time and space. But don't think social studies is just ancient history or only about people in faraway places. And don't panic about memorizing lots of dates and names. Instead, focus on how social studies affects your life every day. After all, savvy girls want the big picture!

Social studies is made up of many subjects, including history, geography, economics, and civics and government, among others. These different subjects are all connected to each other. To see how, think about your favorite pair of jeans. First, people grew the cotton. China, India, and the United States are world leaders in growing cotton. Geography tells you something about where those countries are located and what natural resources they have. For cotton to grow, an area needs fertile soil, sufficient water, and a warm growing season.

The factories that wove the cotton fabric and sewed the jeans may have been in other countries. Check the label, and use a world map to locate the country where your jeans were made.

History helps you learn when and why jeans were invented and how they have changed over the years. History also helps you understand how the cotton industry affected people's lives and contributed to slavery in the United States. History helps you understand the people who made your jeans and their traditions.

Civics and government affect how those people live and their rights as workers. What freedoms do they have? Do they get to choose their government leaders?

Economics deals with all sorts of money issues. Why would a company import your jeans from another country? How much did you pay for the jeans? How much did the cotton farmers earn? What did the factory workers earn? Who else made money?

Just like the threads on your jeans, different strands of social studies are woven together. They all come together to affect our world—and you!

CHAPTER 1

WHERE IN THE WORLD?

Geography deals with an area's physical features and how they affect people's social, political, cultural, and economic lives. It can affect the foods they eat, the jobs they have, and even their hobbies! For example, you might play beach volleyball a lot if you live near the coast in California or Florida. But if you're in West Virginia or Colorado, you might do more hiking or mountain-biking.

Get Social!

Make a poster showing five ways geography affects your life in a typical month. Scan or photograph the poster, and send it to a friend or family member. You could also ask friends to make similar posters and compare how geography affects their lifestyles.

How Tribes Lived

Geography's effect on lifestyles is nothing new. The traditions of American Indian tribes reflected the physical features of their homelands. Eastern Woodland tribes included the Iroquois of New York and the Cherokee of the Southeast. Forests in these areas had plenty of wood for homes and canoes. Animals were also plentiful, which provided meat, along with skins for shoes, clothing, and other uses. Plentiful rainfall allowed tribes to grow corn, squash, and other crops.

The Plains Indians included the Sioux tribe of the Dakotas, the Pawnee of Nebraska, and other Indian groups/nations of the Great Plains. Their prairie homeland supported huge herds of buffalo, along with deer, antelope, and elk. Portable tents or tepees made of animal skins made it easier to follow the herds for hunting.

The Chinook, Tillamook, and other tribes of the Pacific Northwest lived in present-day Oregon and Washington. Coastal waters supplied lots of fish. Forests provided hunting grounds, along with wood for homes and dugout canoes. Totem poles—carvings on long, wooden poles—told about myths and legends.

The Indians of the Southwest included the Hopi, Navajo, and other tribes of Arizona, New Mexico, Colorado, and California. They made their homes from stones or sun-dried bricks called adobe.

Some tribes herded sheep or goats. Irrigation allowed some groups to grow corn.

Inuit tribes in Alaska and northern Canada faced frigid winters. Hunters often wore snowshoes to track moose, caribou, and other Arctic animals for meat. Animal hides were made into tents and warm clothing.

MAPMAKER, MAPMAKER, MAKE ME A MAP

Let's say your soccer team has an away game this weekend. How will you get there? Perhaps your coach handed out directions. If not, you could check a map or use your phone's **Global Positioning System (GPS)**. GPS devices measure the distance from your location to satellites high up in the sky. These satellites orbit Earth and transmit radio signals. Then they use computerized maps to find a route.

Maps have changed throughout history. Early maps often gave rough estimations and were used for trade or exploration. Modern maps show lots of details and help with personal navigation.

There are many kinds of maps and each has a different purpose. For example, political maps show country, state, or local borders.

Suppose you hear a news story about a tornado in a city that you've never heard of. A political map will help you see where the tornado took place.

Topographical maps show what the land looks like. Let's say your family wants to go hiking on an upcoming trip. Topographical maps show if the land is hilly or flat. Are there lakes, rivers, or mountains nearby? Is the area a desert or a lush rain forest?

When packing for your trip, you'll want to know about the upcoming weather. Weather maps show expected high and low temperatures. They also let you know to expect rain, snow, or other kinds of weather.

Get Social!

On your next trip to the grocery store, take a notebook and write down where various foods are from. Perhaps the pineapples came from Hawaii and the bananas from Ecuador. You might find tortillas that were made in Mexico and rice from Thailand. In the dairy aisle, you may find cheese from France or Italy. And don't forget desserts! Chocolate and other sweet treats might be from Belgium or Switzerland.

Use a world map to place stickers of the various foods you found on the countries where they came from. Why do you suppose some products come from particular countries? Geography provides clues.

GREENLAND

The Great Lakes ▶ contain 21 percent of the world's fresh surface water.

NORTH AMERICA

The Sahara Desert sprawls over 3.3 million square miles (8.5 million square km) of northern Africa. The Sahara averages less than 5 inches ▶ (13 centimeters) of rainfall per year.

PACIFIC OCEAN

Earth measures about 25,000 miles (40,234 kilometers) around at the **equator**.

ATLANTIC OCEAN

◀ The Amazon River in South America runs through the world's largest tropical rain forest.

SOUTH AMERICA

Sail On, Jessica!

In 2010 at age 16, Jessica Watson became the youngest person to sail solo around the world. Her nonstop voyage took nearly seven months and covered more than 23,000 nautical miles (26,468 miles/42,596 km).

N
W E
S

ARCTIC
OCEAN

EUROPE

ASIA
The world's 10 tallest mountains
are located in the Himalayan mountain
range in Asia. Mount Everest is the world's
highest peak at 29,029 feet (8,848 meters).
▼

◄ ◄ ◄ ◄ ◄ Africa's Nile River flows
4,175 miles (6,719 km) north
to the Mediterranean Sea.

INDIAN OCEAN

No wonder we call
Earth the Blue Planet!
Oceans cover 71 percent
of Earth's surface and
contain 97 percent of the
planet's water.

AUSTRALIA

The frigid continent of Antarctica
is the world's largest desert.

ANTARCTICA

13

CHAPTER 2

THE OLD, OLD WORLD

Imagine a world without computers, TV, lights, microwaves—or even phones! Suppose there were no cars, trains, or even flush toilets! Yikes! It's hard to imagine, but it wasn't so long ago that people actually survived without those things.

Now imagine going way, way, way back in time. So far, the oldest evidence of modern humans comes from Ethiopia. **Archaeologists** found bones there that are195,000 years old!

Archaeologists have also found bones of earlier ancestors, called **hominids**, in Ethiopia. The most complete hominid skeleton they found was from a female that researchers named "Ardi." Scientists have determined that Ardi lived about 4.4 million years ago, which makes her the oldest human ancestor ever found. Scientists believe Ardi walked upright like humans, but also moved about on all fours in trees, similar to apes.

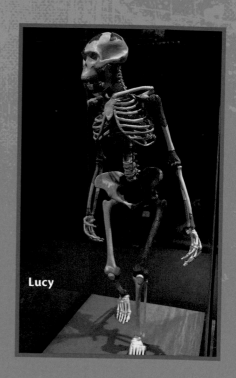

Lucy

Prior to Ardi, "Lucy" was the oldest hominid skeleton ever found. Lucy and her relatives lived 3.2 to 3.6 million years ago. They had a mix of human and apelike features and walked upright. It looks like girls have always ruled!

Roaming Around, Then Settling Down

The world's first people lived by hunting animals and gathering starchy plants, berries, and other foods. Then sometime after 10000 BC, people began farming. They grew grain and other crops. People also started herding sheep and goats. Success in farming allowed towns and cities to grow. In time, people moved all over the world.

FUN FACT

The city of Jericho in the Middle East is more than 10,000 years old. It is perhaps the oldest continuous civilization in the world.

Get Social!

Do some research to find out when your city or town was founded. Why did the first residents decide to settle there? How long have your ancestors lived there? Why does your family live there? Write a blog post to discuss your findings.

IT'S ALL GREEK TO ME

The Greek **city-states** of Sparta and Athens started around 900 BC. From 500 BC to 100 BC, the Greeks ruled a huge empire. Our culture owes a lot to them. Here are just a few of the concepts we got from the ancient Greeks.

Philosophy—Food for Thought

What is the meaning of life? Who are we? Philosophy explores these and other profound questions, and the ancient Greeks definitely had some deep thinkers.

Think your teachers are tough? Socrates—a Greek philosopher who was born in 470 BC—taught by asking tough questions. After each answer, he'd ask even more questions in an attempt to prove his point. He also wanted to make his students contradict their original answers. He did this to get them to realize that they didn't know as much as they thought they did. This is called the Socratic method.

Plato was a student of Socrates. In addition to being a philosopher, he was also a mathematician. He started a school called the Academy that was the first institution of higher learning in the Western world. His idea for good government was to let the philosophers rule!

Democracy

Ancient Greece had many city-states, and Athens was one of the world's first **democracies**. But it wasn't a perfect democracy. All male citizens could vote, but women, slaves, and foreigners could not. Still, it was a start.

The United States is a representative democracy, meaning that voters choose leaders, and those leaders make laws. Do representative democracies affect your school? Does the community elect members of the school board? Do you get to vote for members of the student council?

This theater in Greece survives from ancient times.

Drama

Do you like movies and plays? Ancient Greeks enjoyed the theater too. Comedies had happy endings and often made fun of politics and society. In Aristophanes' play, *Lysistrata*, women went on strike until their husbands agreed to end a war.

Tragedies had sad endings. In 2011 playwright Steven Sater turned Aeschylus' tragedy *Prometheus Bound* into a rock musical.

Sports

In 776 BC the ancient Greeks held the first Olympic games. The ancient games ran for nearly 1,200 years until emperor Theodosius I banned them in AD 393.

The modern Olympic games began in 1896. They still include some track and field events similar to the ancient games, such as the long jump and discus throw. Only men competed in ancient times. But since 1900, women have also participated in the modern Olympics.

ALL ROADS LEAD TO ROME

Just as with the ancient Greeks, our society picked up a few things from the ancient Romans. According to legend, twin brothers Romulus and Remus (who were allegedly raised by a wolf) founded the city of Rome. After a quarrel, Romulus became the city's ruler in 753 BC. Historians aren't sure whether or not this legend is entirely true, but they agree that Rome's roots do reach back that far.

Beginning in 27 BC, Rome built a vast empire. It lasted about 500 years and stretched from western Europe to western Asia and northern Africa. Here are a few things we got from the ancient Romans.

Alphabet

Did you know that you learned to print with Roman letters? That's right! Our alphabet comes from the Romans.

You've probably also seen Roman numerals used on some clocks or watches. Roman numerals are also used in naming each year's Super Bowl. Different letters represent different numbers and are read from left to right to figure out a value. For example, in Roman numerals the year 1776 is MDCCLXXVI. Super Bowl 48 is written Super Bowl XLVIII.

Entertainment

Have you ever been to a concert or sports event at a stadium or coliseum? Rome's Colosseum was a large circular gathering place. Like today's stadiums, it hosted crowds for sports and other forms of entertainment.

The Roman Colosseum was built between AD 70 and 80.

Roads and Public Works

Every day, you travel on roads. You drink water from a faucet. You flush waste down the drain. You go to schools and other public buildings too. In short, you use an infrastructure. An infrastructure is a society's system of basic structures and facilities.

Romans had very basic infrastructures too. They constructed roads. They brought water to cities with **aqueducts**. Some cities even had crude sewer systems in which people threw waste into gutters and rainwater carried it away.

An ancient Roman road

ANCIENT HISTORY IN YOUR LIFE

In addition to the Greeks and Romans, ancient cultures from all over the world invented items that we still use today. From glass to spices to eyeliner, where would we be without the contributions of the ancient world?

Cooking Spices

Do you like spicy food? People in Denmark used garlic mustard around 6,000 years ago. People in ancient India cooked with ginger and turmeric about 4,500 years ago.

Cosmetics

Think beauty products are a modern invention? Think again. Cosmetics have been around for ages. Ancient Egyptians used bold, **kohl** eyeliner. Ancient Greeks, Romans, and Persians used eyeliner too.

Have you ever had a manicure? People in ancient Babylon, China, and Egypt were the first to use nail polish. Even men sometimes colored their nails.

Smelling good was just as important to ancient people as looking good. Perhaps even more so since they had limited sanitation and no modern deodorants. So it's not surprising that people in ancient Babylon, Egypt, Greece, and Rome used perfume to mask offensive odors.

Glass

Ancient Egyptians started using glass furnaces around 1400 BC. The Romans developed the art of blowing glass into different shapes.

Fabrics

Do you love clothes? You know you do! Ancient people did too. Fibers found in the Asian country of Georgia in 2009 were more than 34,000 years old! Archaeologists have also found linen from ancient Turkey and Egypt, silk from ancient China, and cotton from ancient Egypt.

Paper

The ancient Chinese invented paper sometime around 100 BC. But it looked a lot different from the loose-leaf paper you use today. Early papermakers soaked hemp waste, beat it to a pulp, and mixed it with water. Then they suspended it on mesh frames, and let it dry.

Shopping

What savvy girl doesn't like to meet her friends at the mall? Ancient people also used marketplaces to meet up with friends. Large assemblies were held there too. The ancient Greek marketplace was known as the agora. The Roman marketplace was called the forum.

Have you ever had an awful day? Just be grateful you weren't in the Roman city of Pompeii in AD 79. People were going about business as usual when Mount Vesuvius erupted. Many people managed to flee, but hot ash, poisonous gas, and debris killed thousands in the towns near Pompeii.

Until 1748 most of Pompeii stayed buried under ash, just as it had on that fateful day nearly 1,700 years before. Although the eruption of Vesuvius was a disaster for the people of Pompeii, volcanic ash had preserved much of the city. It became a treasure trove for archaeologists who uncovered artifacts such as coins, jewelry, utensils, pots, cups, and sculptures. They even found skeletons that were completely intact.

Beyond that, archaeologists saw how people lived. The people of Pompeii had temples and marketplaces.

Ancient stone streets were home to vendors and food stands. Houses contained garden areas and tiled mosaics. One floor mosaic said, "Cave Canem," which means "Beware of Dog."

Get Social

Imagine that a volcano buried everything in your bedroom for 1,000 years. What artifacts might someone discover in the future? Write a pretend Instagram post about five of those objects. What do they say about you or about how people live today? For example, your cell phone and MP3 player might show others that you're a tech-savvy girl who loves music and taking pics. Share it with your friends, and ask them what their own possible artifacts would be. Discuss the items and whether or not people of the future might misunderstand your generation.

Timeline of the Ancient World

Hominids like Ardi roamed Earth.	Hominids like Lucy and her relatives roamed Earth.	Humans begin farming.	The city of Jericho is founded.
4.4 million years ago	3.2–3.6 million years ago	10000 BC	8000 BC

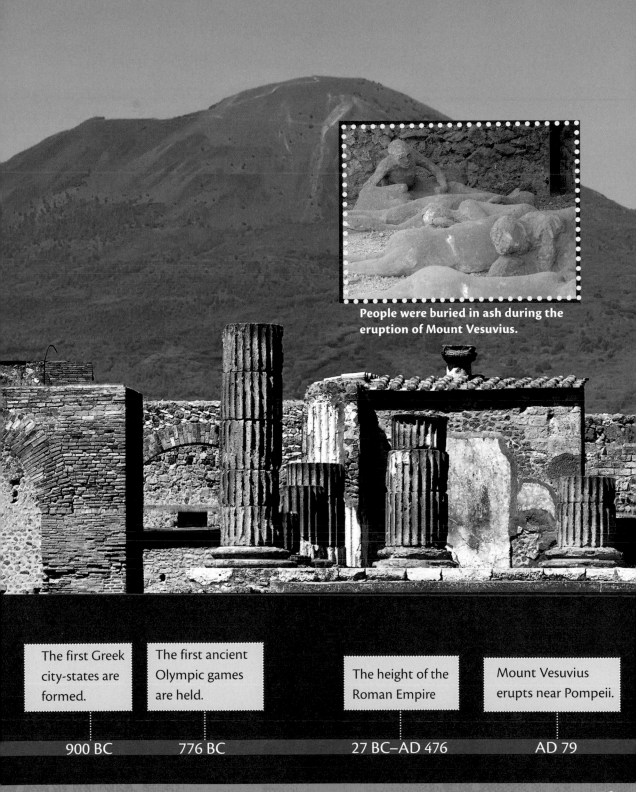

People were buried in ash during the eruption of Mount Vesuvius.

| The first Greek city-states are formed. | The first ancient Olympic games are held. | The height of the Roman Empire | Mount Vesuvius erupts near Pompeii. |
| 900 BC | 776 BC | 27 BC–AD 476 | AD 79 |

GODS, GODDESSES, AND HEROES

So you think your school has angst and drama? That's nothing compared to what went down on Mount Olympus, the home of the ancient Greek gods and goddesses. These mythical celebs often squabbled amongst themselves, and sometimes they interfered in the lives of mortals. Just imagine what the gods and goddesses might say if they were on Facebook or Twitter today.

Zeus (Jupiter)
3 hours ago
My wife, Hera (Juno), is so jealous. Time to throw some thunderbolts and sneak out to see some of my friends.

Leda: Come see me as a swan, Zeus.
2 hours ago

Io: I'm a cow now because of you, Zeus. Stay away from me!
1 hour ago

Hades (Pluto): Have fun, Bro. As usual, I'll be working up a sweat down in the Underworld.
42 minutes ago

Heracles (Hercules): Don't stir up trouble, Dad. Even with my superhuman strength, my plate is full.
11 minutes ago

Athena (Minerva)
2 hours ago
Hmmm ... What should I work on today? War, wisdom, or the arts?

Ares (Mars): I've got warfare covered, if that helps.
48 minutes ago

Ancient Greeks and Romans worshipped many of the same gods. Names in parentheses are the Roman versions.

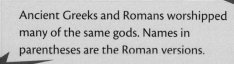

Aphrodite (Venus)

38 minutes ago

Wonder what matchmaking this goddess of love can do today?

Eros (Cupid): I'm all a-quiver to help, Mom. Whom should I shoot with my arrows?

11 minutes ago

Psyche: Hey, Hubby, your mother is plenty powerful already. As the goddess of the soul, I need your help around here today.

7 minutes ago

Demeter (Ceres)

22 minutes ago

Here's to a huge harvest!

Persephone (Proserpina): Way to go, Mom! I'll miss you when I'm vacationing in the Underworld with Hades this winter!

3 minutes ago

Poseidon (Neptune)

8 minutes ago

Got my trident ready to stir up some trouble in the seas.

Perseus: Before you do that, Uncle, could you unchain Andromeda from that rock? If not, I'll have to save her myself.

2 minutes ago

Get Social

Greek gods and goddesses have been characters in many films. Suppose a new movie is in the works. Which Greek god or goddess would you like to play? Write a pretend Twitter post about which role you would want and why. Share it with your friends and ask them to chime in on who they'd want to play.

WORLD RELIGIONS

Does your family celebrate Christmas, observe Passover, fast during Ramadan, or follow other spiritual traditions? If so, you are part of a larger worldwide community. Shared beliefs and traditions give you a common bond with others. Whether you practice a religion or not, learning about other faiths helps you understand other people and the world around you.

Hinduism

Hinduism began in India around 2000 BC. According to Hindus, the gods Brahma, Vishnu, and Shiva create, protect, and destroy the universe.

Dharma is the Hindu concept of duty and morality. Karma is the idea that every action causes an effect, whether now or later. It's the idea that what goes around comes around.

Judaism

Jewish people believe in one God who made a covenant, or promise, to his people. They believe God revealed his will to Abraham, Moses, and other prophets. Judaism began in the Middle East around 2000 BC. Jesus and his family were Jewish, but followers of Judaism do not believe that Jesus was the Son of God. Even so, the first five books of the Christian Bible (the Old Testament) come from the Jewish Torah.

Christianity

Christianity began in present-day Israel about 2,000 years ago. Christians believe in one God with three aspects—God the Father, Jesus the Son, and the Holy Spirit.

Christians believe that Jesus died on a cross to make up for human sins. Christians further believe that Jesus rose from the dead and that they will be with God in heaven after death.

Buddhism

Buddhists see the desire for worldly things as the ultimate cause of suffering. Like Hindus, they believe in the ideas of dharma and karma. Buddhism began when Siddhartha Gautama began teaching in India around 525 BC. Buddhists follow the Noble Eightfold Path as they seek enlightenment, or nirvana.

Islam

Islam's followers, called Muslims, believe in one God named Allah. They believe Allah revealed his teachings to Muhammad, who lived from AD 570 to AD 632 in the area that is now Saudi Arabia. Muhammad's teachings are in Islam's holy book, the Qur'an. Muslims strive to live by the five Pillars of Islam, which deal with faith, prayer, charity, fasting, and making a pilgrimage.

Get Social!

Make a greeting card for a religious holiday outside your own faith. Show that you know what the holiday is about and how people celebrate it.

CHAPTER 3

THEN AND NOW

Chances are your life is much different now than when you were a baby. You've grown taller, learned to walk, talk, and read. And more changes are yet to come. Similarly, society has changed by leaps and bounds from how it was hundreds of years ago. Yet many traditions, ideas, and social issues are still relevant today.

The Feudal System = Rigid

So you think your school's cliques can be rigid? School cliques are a piece of cake compared to Europe in the **Middle Ages**. Back then, birth decided who you were and what you did. Period. End of story.

Here's what happened. Over time, the Roman Empire became too huge to rule easily, so it split into two parts. But economic troubles and political corruption were major problems. By AD 500 the Roman Empire had crumbled.

After the fall of the Roman Empire, Europe had no strong central government. And there were literally barbarians at the gate. Attacking groups included the Huns, Vandals, and the Goths. (These were the original Goths, and it's unlikely they wore gobs of black eye makeup and combat boots.)

Like vandals today, the original Vandals and other barbarians looted places. The feudal system developed as a means of protection.

Unlike cliques at school, everyone owed something to a group in the feudal system. But similar to cliques, some groups fared much better than others. Today's "alpha males" and "queen bees" are much like lords in the feudal system. They are at the top of the food chain.

WANTED!

So who was who in the feudal system? If there were want ads for members of the feudal system, here's what they might have said:

Lords Wanted

Do you own lots of land for an estate? Would you like hundreds of people supporting your lifestyle? In return, your army must protect the people at your castle when danger threatens. And you will owe a duty of loyalty to the king. Only the oldest male heir of a prior lord can apply.

Other Nobles Needed

Men, use your management skills to oversee parts of the lord's estate, or do other high-level work for the lord. Women, be part of the "in" crowd as ladies-in-waiting for the lord's wife. Help her run the household, keep her company, and do sewing or other jobs for her. Only members of the nobility need apply.

Train to Be a Knight in Shining Armor!

Do you love a good fight? Think you'd look great in **chain mail** or a suit of armor? Then work your way up from page to squire to knight. Only male children of nobility may apply. Must be at least 7 years old.

Work for God: Become a Member of the Clergy

Feeling holy? As a priest, nun, or monk, you'll serve in the church. Pray throughout the day and night. You might also read, study, write, and run a business on church lands. Nobility strongly preferred.

FUN FACT

Medieval castles did not have running water, so many people used **chamber pots**. But some castles had bathrooms called garderobes. They were like indoor port-a-potties, and waste dropped down below to the lowest floor.

Serfs or Peasants

If you're not a craftsperson or a member of the noble class, then this is the perfect job for you! (Actually, it's pretty much the only job for you.) Get plenty of fresh air as you toil long hours on a farm. You can even work inside the castle! There you can empty chamber pots, work in the kitchen, clean the castle, or muck out the stables. Women, you get to do double duty. Besides your other tasks, you can keep house and care for the children.

Bayeux Tapestry

Made in the 1070s, the Bayeux Tapestry isn't a heavy rug used to fight drafts inside a castle. It's a 230-foot (70-m) long piece of cloth with embroidered pictures that show how William the Conqueror defeated England in 1066. The tapestry is on display at a museum in Normandy, France.

Get Social!

You can make your own personal "tapestry." Start by pasting together a few pieces of poster board to make one long sheet. On the paper, draw pictures about key events in your life. You can also add copies of some of your favorite photographs. Then connect the events with a timeline on the bottom of the tapestry.

If you're feeling particularly artistic, you could use fabric markers to draw your key events on a T-shirt or pillowcase. Be sure to put waxed paper inside the shirt or pillowcase so the markers don't bleed through.

31

WOMEN'S WORK

What career do you want to have when you grow up? You'll have many choices, but that wasn't always the case. Even in the United States today, men hold most of the jobs in some fields, such as construction. In fields such as nursing and administrative work, women still hold the majority of the jobs.

Medieval towns had lots of jobs for craftspeople. Children started as apprentices. After several years of apprenticeship, they could become journeymen and work for other people. A few became master craftsmen and ran their own businesses. Guilds were unions that helped craftspeople learn their trade and get ahead.

However, some guilds were guys-only clubs that barred women entirely. Some guilds only let in women if their husbands died, and they took over the business.

Goldsmiths, shoemakers, and bookbinders were a few guilds that allowed both male and female members. There were also a few women-only guilds, such as the spinners or silk weavers.

Whether they were in a guild or not, wives often worked alongside husbands in their crafts. Women worked in the fields along with other family members. In addition, they took care of children, cleaned, and cooked. Whew!

Get Social!

Women still lead only a minority of America's top businesses. Go online and find a company whose president or chief executive officer (CEO) is a woman. See if you can follow her on Twitter. If she has a blog, follow that too! You might just learn some savvy business advice from a female trailblazer.

The U.S. government used the image of Rosie the Riveter to encourage women to enter the workforce when World War II (1939–1945) caused labor shortages.

A RENAISSANCE IN THE
Arts

Has your school faced funding cuts for art and music? Things were quite different during the **Renaissance**. Back then, artists started focusing on things other than church art. They painted and sculpted people and events from ancient Greece and Rome.

The music scene also went through major changes. New instruments were invented, including the viola, recorder, and harpsichord. In modern times, music trends change every few years. Just think about how different the music you listen to is from the music your parents or grandparents grew up with.

Advances took place in science and technology too. In 1448 Johannes Gutenberg invented the printing press, which enabled books to be mass-produced. Without it, you wouldn't be able to read your favorite books. His invention was as important to the Renaissance as the Internet is to modern times. Both inventions enabled knowledge and ideas to spread more easily.

Get Social!

What's your favorite form of art? Do you like to draw, paint, or take photographs? Do you play music, sing, or dance? Do you sew, make jewelry, or do other crafts? Do you write poetry, plays, or stories? Make a poster about your favorite type of creative expression to try to persuade others to try it. Do some research on different forms of Renaissance art and creative expression. Then compare or contrast how alike or different your favorite form of expression was back then.

The Industrial Revolution

Are you a tech-savvy girl who keeps up with new gadgets and apps? These days, technology is changing at a lightning-fast rate. But technological advances are nothing new. In the 1700s and 1800s, factories made things that were previously made in home or in shops.

Innovations from the Industrial Revolution continue to impact us today. For proof, just take a quick look in your closet. Most likely, all your clothes were made in a factory. Even if you have some handmade clothes, the fabric or the yarn probably came from a factory.

Some machines invented during the Industrial Revolution performed basic tasks. For example, Eli Whitney's cotton gin cleaned cotton from the fields.

Other inventions provided power, such as James Watt's steam engine. Robert Fulton's steamboat and other inventions improved transportation.

Factory work was hard and often dangerous. By the 1840s workers were demanding better wages and hours. They also wanted safer workplaces. But it would be a long time before change would come. In fact by 1890, full-time factory workers labored an average of 100 hours per week.

Finally in 1933 the National Industrial Recovery Act set a national minimum wage and maximum weekly work hours. That means when you get your first job, there's a certain amount that you must be paid. This law also gave U.S. workers the right to bargain through unions.

Mill Girls

Children and teens had long worked on farms. During the Industrial Revolution, they went to work in factories that used some of the newly invented machines. In Massachusetts, textile mills hired many teen girls. For 12 hours a day, six days a week, these girls toiled in the factories. Many of these "mill girls" earned less than $1 a day.

CHAPTER 4

A WORLD VIEW

Every day you get up, grab some breakfast, and head to school. After a long day of learning, you squeeze in time for sports, music, or other activities. Many kids around the world follow similar schedules, just with different foods, classes, and activities.

It was the same way back in the Middle Ages. During that time, cultures in India, China, and the Middle East not only existed but thrived. For example, movable type was invented in China around AD 1040—about 400 years before Gutenberg invented the printing press! The Chinese also created the first government-issued paper money around this time.

Trade also flourished. The Silk Road was a series of trade routes that stretch 4,000 miles (6,437 km) from China to the Mediterranean Sea. Silk was the major product traded along the route, but other items were also exchanged.

Lots of things were also happening in North and South America. Europeans just didn't know about them yet.

FUN FACT

"Baby, you're a firework!" Around the year AD 1000—way before Katy Perry sang those inspirational lyrics—the Chinese invented gunpowder and fireworks.

Christopher Columbus

A New World

Have you ever taken a school trip to a museum, amusement park, or other tourist attraction? Before you went, did you check out the attraction's website or find out more about the city where you were going? We're lucky enough to plan ahead and learn about where we're going. Early explorers didn't have that luxury.

In the late 1400s and early 1500s, Christopher Columbus, Hernán Cortés, and other Spanish explorers introduced the "New World" to Europe. They inspired others to make the journey. However, these explorers did not discover the New World. It was already inhabited by native people, and their explorations had devastating effects on the lives and cultures of these native populations. But many ideas from their cultures live on today.

Meet the Mayas

The Mayan culture thrived in Mexico and Central America for thousands of years, reaching its peak between AD 250 and 1500 BC. The Mayas were known for their architecture, such as pyramids, statues, and temples. They also had their own writing system of hieroglyphs—the first written language in the Americas. The Mayas formed their own numbering system, and they made extremely accurate astrological observations, upon which their calendar was based. They also enjoyed playing and watching ball games that were similar to racquetball or handball—only much more brutal and sometimes ending in death.

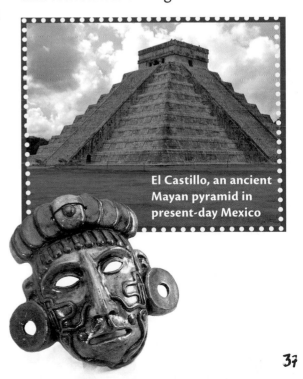
El Castillo, an ancient Mayan pyramid in present-day Mexico

Amazing Aztecs

What does chocolate have to do with social studies? Some favorite Mexican dishes come from the ancient Aztecs, including enchiladas, tacos, and guacamole. The words "chocolate," "tomato," and "chili" all come from the Aztec language.

The Aztecs ruled a vast empire from the 1200s until 1521 when they were conquered by Spanish explorer Hernán Cortés. Mexico City is located on the site where Tenochtitlán—the capital city of the Aztec empire—once stood. Like the Mayas, the Aztecs were also noted for their art and architecture. Two of the most famous surviving sites include Templo Mayor, one of the Aztecs' main temples, and Tenayuca, an ancient pyramid. Both are located near present-day Mexico City.

The ruins of several pyramids and temples are located in Teotihuacan, about 30 miles (48 km) northeast of Mexico City. This includes the Pyramid of the Sun, which is the third largest pyramid in the world. It dates back to around AD 100.

Intriguing Incas

The Inca civilization began in Peru in the 1200s. It was the largest empire in the Americas prior to the arrival of European settlers. It stretched across 2,500 miles (4,023 km) through western South America.

Like the Aztecs and Mayas, architecture was important to the Incas. Perhaps the most famous site of Inca ruins is Machu Picchu. This sanctuary was built in the mid-1400s. It sits high in the Andes Mountains, 7,972 feet (2,430 m) above sea level. All of its incredible buildings and stonework were made without modern tools! Because the Spanish were unaware of Machu Picchu's existence, it survived when the Spanish destroyed much of the Inca empire in 1572.

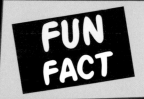

FUN FACT

Sometime around 5000 BC, the Chinchorro Indians of South America made the world's earliest known mummies. They stuffed dead family members' bodies with straw.

A COUNTRY OF IMMIGRANTS

After Columbus arrived in America, many changes took place. People began moving to the New World from around the globe. Some came for political or religious freedom. From 1881 until after World War II (1939–1945), religious **persecution** drove many Jewish people from Russia, Eastern Europe, and Germany.

Natural disasters and economic hardships also cause people to leave their homeland and sail to the United States. Ireland suffered a potato famine from 1845 to 1849. Between 1845 and 1855, about 1.5 million Irish people came to the United States.

The Plight of American Indians

American Indians were already in America when Europeans arrived. The Europeans brought diseases and tried to get the American Indians to change their beliefs, customs, and lifestyles. They also forced some Indians to leave their homes and move to **reservations**.

Some **immigrants** sought better job prospects. Others came for a good education. But moving from one country to another is rarely easy. Prejudice makes things difficult. Some groups fear newcomers will take away jobs. Others don't trust people who come from different cultures or have different religious beliefs. They often forget that their own family members were once newcomers too.

Get Social!

Trace your family tree. How far back can you go? Where did your ancestors come from?

Get Social!

Today many communities celebrate their diversity. Ethnic festivals and other events draw big crowds. And everyone enjoys some sort of ethnic food!

Plan an international potluck party. Make invitations and ask friends or family members to bring foods from different countries. During the party, have each guest talk briefly about the country that their food represents.

THE PERILS OF WAR

The United States avoided foreign wars for most of the 1800s. Since then, it has fought in several wars. Two of them were so widespread that they became world wars.

World War I (1914–1918)

Do you ever feel as if friends are drawing you into arguments that you'd rather not be a part of? That's kind of what happened with World War I.

For about 40 years, political tensions had run high in Europe. Different treaties bound countries to back each other up in case of war. Then an assassin killed Austria-Hungary's Archduke Franz Ferdinand in Sarajevo, which was then part of Serbia.

What followed was like a house of cards collapsing. First, Austria-Hungary declared war against Serbia. Then other countries got into the act, backing up each other's allies.

American soldiers march through France on their way to battle during World War I.

As the war went on, Germany attacked American ships going to Europe. In 1917 the United States joined the war on the side of France, Great Britain, Serbia, and their allies.

In the end, Great Britain, France, the United States, Russia, and their allies won the war. The Central Powers of Germany, Austria-Hungary, Bulgaria, and the Ottoman Empire lost. The war killed more than 8 million people and wounded over 21 million.

Trench warfare was used prominently during World War I.

We celebrate Veterans Day on November 11 because that's the anniversary of the end of fighting in World War I.

World War II (1939-1945)

Everyone makes mistakes and does things they regret in life. But it's important to learn from those mistakes and to not make them again. That's one reason why it's important to study history—so we learn from the tragedies of the past. And World War II was a tragic situation.

Combine a bleak economic situation, territorial greed, and resentment after World War I, and you have the makings for another war. Add a crazed leader aiming to control the world, and the fuse was lit for World War II.

World War II officially began when German leader Adolf Hitler had his troops invade Poland in 1939. Throughout the war, Hitler's **Nazi** regime imprisoned and murdered millions of Jewish people. Approximately 6 million Jewish people perished in what became known as the Holocaust.

Hitler gives his trademark salute during a Nazi party rally.

American troops storm a beach in the Pacific during World War II.

The United States didn't immediately enter the war. But on December 7, 1941, the Japanese bombed Pearl Harbor in Hawaii, which was then a U.S. territory. After that, the United States then entered the war immediately, sending troops to battle in both Europe and the Pacific.

Warring countries fell into two "teams." Great Britain, France, the United States, Russia, and other countries eventually won as the Allies. Germany, Italy, and Japan were the losing Axis Powers.

About 15 million people died in battle, and another 25 million were wounded. About 45 million more people died as civilians, although sources vary.

Get Social!

Has someone you know served in the armed forces? Interview that individual in person or by phone. Find out what it was like for them to serve their country. Afterward, write a note to that person thanking him or her for the hard work and sacrifices made in defending our nation.

REMEMBER OUR VETERANS

CHAPTER 5

WE THE PEOPLE

If you form a club at school, you need rules. The United States needs rules too. The U.S. Constitution is our nation's set of rules. It's the supreme law of the land and has been in force since 1789. Since then, 27 **amendments** have been added.

The Constitution separates powers among three branches of government— legislative, executive, and judiciary. The legislative branch is made up of senators and representatives who make laws. The executive branch enforces those laws. And the courts in the judicial branch explain the meaning of those laws. No branch rules the country alone. Instead, a system of checks and balances gives each branch certain procedures to keep the others in line.

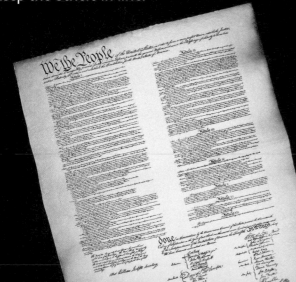

Congress: The Legislative Branch

"A woman's place is in the House ... and in the Senate." This saying is more than just a T-shirt slogan. It's a call for girls and women to get into politics. And it's a reminder that Congress has two parts—the Senate and the House of Representatives.

The Senate has 100 members— two from each state—who serve for six-year terms. The House of Representatives has 435 members. The number from each state depends on its population, which changes every 10 years based on the official census. Members of the House serve two-year terms.

Congress makes the laws for the country. Each law starts out when a congressperson introduces a **bill**. Members of the House or Senate debate or talk about the pros and cons of the bill, and sometimes they make changes to it.

Finally the members of Congress vote on the bill. In order for it to become a law, the bill must get a majority of votes from both the House and Senate.

The Bill of Rights

The first 10 constitutional amendments, known as the Bill of Rights, were approved in 1791. The Bill of Rights defines some of our most basic rights, including:

1. In the United States, you can speak freely, read newspapers and magazines, gather in groups, and practice whatever religion you want. You can even complain about the government if you want. We have the First Amendment to thank for those rights.

2. The Second Amendment gives citizens the right to own guns.

3. Don't want uninvited guests? According to the Third Amendment, you don't have to let soldiers stay in your home or eat your food.

4. Because of the Fourth Amendment, the police can't just barge into your house, go through your stuff, and take it. In order to do so, they need a search warrant and a good reason, like suspecting that you committed a crime.

5. The Fifth Amendment says you can only be charged once for a crime. The government also can't make you say anything against yourself. When someone says, "I plead the fifth," they're referring to their right not to **incriminate** themselves.

6. Do you ever watch crime shows on TV? The trial scenes are dramatic, and real trials are too. Under the Sixth Amendment, if you're charged with a crime, you have the right to a trial as soon as possible. You also have the right to tell your side of the story and can have a lawyer defend you. At your trial, a jury will decide whether you are guilty or not.

7. According to the Seventh Amendment, you can have a jury decide most civil cases, which are disputes over property or a lot of money.

8. Thanks to the Eighth Amendment, the government can't punish you in cruel ways. You also can't be charged an unreasonable amount of money for bail or fines.

9. Want the right to more rights? The Ninth Amendment says that these aren't the only rights U.S. citizens have. So just because they aren't specifically mentioned here doesn't mean you don't have other rights. The right to privacy is one example.

10. If the Constitution doesn't specifically say states can't do something then according to the Tenth Amendment, they have the power to do so. Many matters dealing with property law fall into this category.

When both houses finally agree, the bill goes to the president. If the president signs it, the bill becomes a law. But the president has the power to veto, or reject, any bill. Even if the president vetoes it, a bill can still become a law if two-thirds of both houses vote for it again.

Congress also has some control over presidential power. If Congress doesn't like what the president or the executive agencies do, it can withhold funding. This check is called the "power of the purse." You've probably experienced this at home when you wanted something that your parents didn't want you to have. Perhaps you wanted a flashy new cell phone, but your parents—who held the purse strings—said no.

Get Social!

What laws would you liked to see changed? Would you like to see age restrictions for social media sites lowered or dropped altogether? How do you feel about the ratings system for movies? Express your opinion in a letter or e-mail to your senator or representative. Use your skills to persuade him or her to see your point of view. Be sure to use persuasive language, supporting details, and facts to back up your opinion.

The Executive Branch

The President heads the executive branch. Its agencies carry out and enforce the laws. The president has other jobs too, including:

➤ representing America to the world.
➤ directing foreign policy, which is how America interacts with other countries.
➤ commanding the armed forces. However, only Congress can formally declare war.
➤ signing or vetoing laws passed by Congress.
➤ drafting laws and sending them to members of Congress to introduce as bills.

Get Social!

Suppose you were running for president. What issues are important to you? Ending hunger and homelessness? Achieving world peace? Affordable health care for all U.S. citizens? Design an ad to persuade people to vote for you based on the issues you support. Or, if there's a presidential election coming up, see if you can organize a mock election at your school or in your class.

THE ELECTORAL COLLEGE

Every four years, voters see presidential candidates' names on the ballot, but the person with the most votes doesn't necessarily become president. You may be wondering, "How can this be? We live in a democratic society where we get to choose our leaders!" And you're right. But during presidential elections, U.S. citizens are really choosing a group of electors.

Electors are people who make up the Electoral College. Under the Constitution, the Electoral College votes for who becomes president.

For most states, the candidate with the most votes in a state receives all the state's electoral votes. (Maine and Nebraska have a different system.) Candidates need 270 of the total 538 electoral votes to win.

Election 2000

Usually, the candidate who receives the most votes in the popular election becomes president. But that wasn't the case in 2000. That year Democratic candidate Al Gore received about 500,000 more popular votes than Republican George W. Bush. But because of the states he won, Bush received 271 votes in the Electoral College and became the country's 43rd president.

2000 Presidential election returns

Popular vote	
Al Gore	50,158,094
George W. Bush	49,820,518

Electoral vote	
George W. Bush	271
Al Gore	267

The Judicial Branch

The judicial branch is a system of courts. It's the courts' job to make sure laws follow the Constitution. The Supreme Court is the highest court in the United States. Each year the Supreme Court hears arguments in about 100 of the approximately 10,000 cases it is asked to review. The Supreme Court takes a look at how the laws are applied in these cases and whether they follow the Constitution. The Supreme Court's nine justices have the final word on what the Constitution and federal laws mean.

Supreme Court justices and other federal judges can serve for life. Because they don't worry about re-election, federal judges can focus more on the law, instead of politics.

Want to be a "Supreme"? You'll have to overcome some hurdles before you do. First, the president must nominate, or name, someone to fill an open position in the Supreme Court. Then a majority of the Senate needs to agree with the president's choice. This is called confirming the candidate. These steps let the other two branches of government shape the courts' makeup. That can sway how courts decide cases.

FUN FACT

The Supreme Court very rarely holds trials, but it is possible. If one state sues another, for example, the case can start out in the Supreme Court. In 1998 a Supreme Court case dealt with a dispute between New York and New Jersey about who owned Ellis Island.

Get Social!

Should the United States keep the Electoral College? Or should it amend the Constitution so that whichever candidate gets the most popular votes becomes president? Ask at least 25 people what they think. Show the poll results on a bar graph.

FEDERALISM AT SCHOOL

So if the three branches of the national government follow a system of checks and balances, why do we also need state governments? The answer is **federalism**.

In the United States, some things are solely the job of the national government, such as making money or running the army. Authority for a few issues rests solely with the states. For example, each state can decide the minimum age for getting a driver's license. The federal and state governments share authority in many other areas, such as environmental matters and health law.

You may not realize it, but the federal, state, and local governments affect you every day, even at school. Here's how:

➤ State and local governments tell teachers what to teach in each grade. The government sets requirements for what you need to learn to move up to the next grade and graduate.

➤ The federal government says that all children have the right to a free public school education. Period. The law says that no matter what a child's skin color or religion, he or she cannot be denied an education.

➤ Your parents aren't the only ones concerned about your safety at school. Products in the gym, on the playground, and elsewhere in schools must meet safety standards set by the federal government.

GIRLS RULE!

Can you believe that women didn't have the right to vote nationwide until 1920? Even so, that didn't stop Jeannette Rankin of Montana from becoming the first woman in Congress in 1917. Nellie Tayloe Ross of Wyoming became the first woman governor in 1925. Two weeks later, Miriam "Ma" Ferguson became the first woman governor of Texas.

Since then, hundreds of women have served in state and federal government. In 1969 Shirley Chisholm became America's first black congresswoman. Sandra Day O'Connor became the first woman on the Supreme Court in 1981.

Condoleezza Rice and Madeleine Albright both served as secretary of state. Elizabeth Dole was secretary of transportation, secretary of labor, and a senator. After serving as First Lady of the United States from 1993–2000, Hillary Clinton became a senator and then secretary of state. She even ran for president.

Nellie Tayloe Ross

Marion Glass Banister

Get Social!

Pretend you're interviewing for your dream job in government. What job would you want? Suppose you are asked why you want the job and why you'd be the right person for the job. Write a paragraph to answer their questions. Be sure to talk about your major in college and your previous jobs on your climb up the career ladder.

Women leaders have ruled in countries around the
world too. Here are a few female leaders from modern times:

Indira Gandhi

prime minister of India, 1966–1977, 1980–1984

Golda Meir

prime minister of Israel, 1969–1974

Margaret Thatcher

prime minister of Great Britain, 1979–1990

Angela Merkel

chancellor of Germany, starting in 2005

Dilma Rousseff

president of Brazil, starting in 2011

FUN FACT
More than 300 million people
live in the United States, and
the country is still growing!

CHAPTER 6

EQUALITY FOR ALL

Have you ever felt discriminated against? Has anyone ever told you that you couldn't do something simply because you're a girl? If so, that's discrimination.

The Declaration of Independence says "all men are created equal." But for much of the nation's history, that line was interpreted to mean "all white men." For many years, nonwhite men and women of any color were not given the same rights as white men.

Until 1865 slavery was a way of life in some states. The 13th amendment put an end to that, but many states still discriminated against African-Americans.

Private businesses discriminated too. Some businesses wouldn't hire people of certain races, religions, or ethnic groups. Other companies wouldn't give them the same service that others received.

Women also suffered discrimination. Even after women nationwide won the right to vote in 1920, some states limited women's right to own property. Some firms wouldn't hire or promote women. Many companies didn't pay them as much as men.

FUN FACT

Abraham Lincoln made a clear link between democracy and equality when he said, "As I would not be a slave, so I would not be a master. This is my idea of democracy. Whatever differs from this, to the extent of the difference, is no democracy."

Six constitutional amendments expanded civil rights:

- ➤➤ 1865: The 13th Amendment ended slavery.
- ➤➤ 1868: The 14th Amendment guaranteed equal protection under the law.
- ➤➤ 1870: The 15th Amendment said states can't deny citizens the right to vote because of their race.
- ➤➤ 1920: The 19th Amendment gave women the right to vote nationwide.
- ➤➤ 1964: The 24th Amendment banned poll taxes that kept people from voting.
- ➤➤ 1971: The 26th Amendment lowered the national voting age to 18.

Federal laws also helped make equality a reality. The Civil Rights Act of 1964 says businesses, schools, and other places can't discriminate because of race, religion, or gender. The law also forbids job discrimination based on these factors.

Other important civil rights laws include the Voting Rights Act of 1965, the Fair Housing Act of 1968, the Age Discrimination in Employment Act of 1967, and the Americans with Disabilities Act of 1990.

Before Congress passed these laws, men, women, and even children banded together to call for change. They used their constitutional rights to change unfair and unjust laws. They wrote to lawmakers. They held public meetings. They spoke out for their beliefs— sometimes at great personal cost.

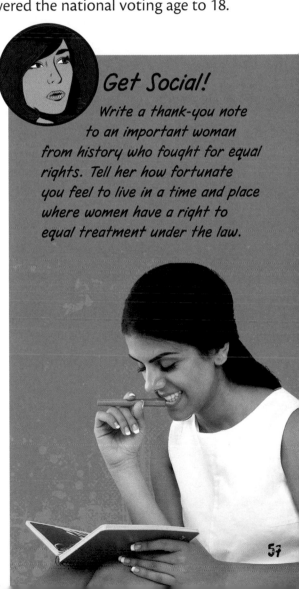

Get Social!

Write a thank-you note to an important woman from history who fought for equal rights. Tell her how fortunate you feel to live in a time and place where women have a right to equal treatment under the law.

GIRLS GO TO COURT

Some important Supreme Court cases have involved kids like you. In 1951 an African-American girl named Linda Brown couldn't go to the school closest to her home. The board of education for Topeka, Kansas, said it was for white students only. Because of segregation, Linda had to walk six blocks and then take a bus to a school for black children.

Her parents and some others sued. The case, *Brown v. Board of Education*, went all the way to the Supreme Court. In 1954 the Supreme Court said that racially segregated schools are unequal. They violated the 14th Amendment right to equal protection under the law.

In 1965 an Iowa school suspended three students for wearing black armbands to protest the Vietnam War. John and Mary Beth Tinker, Chris Eckhardt, and their parents sued, and the case went to the Supreme Court.

In 1969 the Court ruled in the students' favor. The Court said the students weren't disrupting school activities or interfering with anyone else's rights. Therefore, the school violated the students' First Amendment rights to freedom of speech and expression.

Mary Beth and John Tinker

Get Social!

Pretend you're Linda Brown or Mary Beth Tinker. Write a fictional Facebook post about your court victory. Add comments that you might get from others. How would you respond to their comments?

Get Social!

Research some charitable groups in your community. Choose one and ask your parents about volunteering there. Helping others makes your community better for everyone. It will make you feel good too.

Malala Makes a Difference

You don't have to hold a government job to inspire and lead people. Pakistani teen Malala Yousafzai spoke out for girls' rights to an education. She kept speaking out even after Taliban terrorists tried to kill her.

In Pakistan girls are sometimes banned from going to school. In 2009 when Malala was just 11 years old, she started writing a blog. In her blog she discussed her life under Taliban rule and her views on education for girls. About a year later, a documentary was made about her life. After that, she began giving interviews and was even nominated for the International Children's Peace Prize.

But in 2012 members of the Taliban shot her in the head while she was riding on a school bus. She survived and went on to gain worldwide recognition, becoming a spokesperson for children's education. She was even nominated for a Nobel Peace Prize. When she spoke at the United Nations in 2013 she said, "One child, one teacher, one book, and one pen can change the world."

THE CHALLENGES AHEAD

Social studies past and present continue to shape our world. And whether you realize it or not, social studies is all around you. It connects people across time and space. Through e-mail, blogs, and social networks, the world seems to be a much smaller place today. You can connect with people—whether they're across town or across the world—in a matter of seconds.

Despite this sense of togetherness, many poorer countries are facing serious issues, such as poverty, drought, hunger, and natural disasters. Restrictions on women also cause broader problems. Women without equal opportunities have less power to help themselves and their families. Some restrictions also leave women more vulnerable to violence or disease.

The world won't solve these problems overnight, but education is the first step. Follow the news. Keep up on current events. Read about different cultures too. Use a blog or social media site to express your opinion on issues that interest you. Whatever method you choose, find a way to get involved. What happens now will become the history of tomorrow. Your actions DO make a difference!

GLOSSARY

amendment (uh-MEND-muhnt)—a change made to a law or a legal document

aqueduct (AK-wuh-duhkt)—a large bridge built to carry water from a mountain into the valley

archaeologist (ar-kee-OL-uh-jist)—someone who studies how people lived in the past

bill (BIL)—a proposed law introduced in Congress

chain mail (CHAYN MAYL)—armor made up of thousands of tiny iron rings linked together

chamber pot (CHAYM-buhr POT)—a type of bowl that people used as a toilet

city-state (SI-tee STAYT)—a self-governing community including a town and its surrounding territory

democracy (di-MAH-kruh-see)—a form of government in which the citizens can choose their leaders

equator (i-KWAY-tur)—an imaginary line around the middle of Earth; it divides the northern and southern hemispheres

federalism (FED-ur-uhl-iz-um)—a political system that binds a group of states into a larger, superior state while allowing them to maintain their own identities

Global Positioning System (GPS) (GLOH-buhl puh-ZI-shuh-ning SISS-tuhm)—an electronic tool used to find the location of an object on Earth

hominid (HOM-i-nid)—two-footed primate mammals that include human beings and their extinct ancestors and related forms

immigrant (IM-uh-gruhnt)—a person who moves from one country to live permanently in another

incriminate (in-KRIM-uh-nate)—to show that someone is guilty of a crime or another wrong action

kohl (KOL)—a cosmetic used by women to darken the edges of the eyelids

medieval (mee-DEE-vuhl)—having to do with the Middle Ages

Middle Ages (MID-uhl AY-jiz)—the period of European history between approximately AD 500 and 1450 BC

Nazi (NOT-see)—the German political party led by Adolph Hitler; the Nazis ruled Germany from 1933 to 1945.

persecution (pur-suh-KYOO-shun)—cruel or unfair treatment, often because of race or religious beliefs

Renaissance (REN-uh-sahnss)—a period in Europe beginning in the 14th century and ending in mid-17th century that is noted for its cultural achievements

reservation (rez-er-VAY-shuhn)—an area of land set aside by the U.S. government for American Indians

READ MORE

Adams, Simon. *The Kingfisher Atlas of World History*. New York: Kingfisher, 2010.

Brasch, Nicolas. *The Industrial Revolution: Age of Invention*. Discovery Education: Discoveries and Inventions. New York: PowerKids Press, 2014.

Friedman, Mark. *The Democratic Process*. Cornerstones of Freedom. New York: Children's Press, 2012.

Tougas, Shelley. *Girls Rule!: Amazing Tales of Female Leaders*. Savvy: Girls Rock! North Mankato, Minn.: Capstone Press, 2014.

INTERNET SITES

FactHound offers a safe, fun way to find Internet sites related to this book. All of the sites on FactHound have been researched by our staff.

Here's all you do:

Visit *www.facthound.com*

Type in this code: 9781491407752

Super-cool stuff! Check out projects, games and lots more at **www.capstonekids.com**

INDEX